It Began

Poems

by

Michael Jemal

BLUE LIGHT PRESS ◆ 1ST WORLD PUBLISHING

1ST WORLD PUBLISHING

SAN FRANCISCO ◆ FAIRFIELD ◆ DELHI

Winner, 2023 Blue Light Poetry Prize

It Began

Copyright ©2024 by Michael Jemal

1st World Library
PO Box 2211
Fairfield, IA 52556
www.1stworldpublishing.com

Blue Light Press
www.bluelightpress.com
bluelightpress@aol.com

Book & Cover Design
Melanie Gendron
melaniegendron999@gmail.com

Cover Art
copyright-free fantasy art
clipground.com

Author Photo
Priscilla Cintron

First Edition

Library of Congress Cataloging-in-Publication Data

ISBN: 978-1-4218-3562-4

It Began

For Priscilla and Jakob.

Also, thanks to Brian Overall for his support.

It was a night like all the others.
Empty of everything save memory.
He thought he got to the other side of things.
But he hadn't.

– Raymond Carver

Prologue

It began when I accidentally
stepped on your left foot
and you broke
into a million excuses.

What good is love without a few
hazard lights flashing.

Here's something that might calm you.
I'm not who I say
I am.
I've been patching myself together
for years.
I'm brand new.

If I put on my best pants
will you dance with me tonight.
I have so many stories in my pocket
I need to unwind.
Have you ever seen
inside the body
of a meaningful thought.
There are so many shades of despair,
I'm almost ready to shout.

1

It began the night my shadow
dressed up to go out without me
and never returned
and I was left undone,
piece by piece.
My body had forgotten
how to sleep.
I'd walk about the apartment
aimlessly throughout the days and nights
hoping to find
all the pieces that had fallen off me.
There was no way to know
when I opened the door to the bathroom
and stood in front of mirror
I would wonder
who was looking at me.

2

It began after five days of rain
when I decided to live elsewhere
because I could not escape
my assorted contradictions.
I was in the world
but separate from it.
I had to teach myself how to lie
with my eyes wide open.
I had been guilty
of blindness for so long,
my hair changed color.
I needed a hallucination
I could feel good about.
Shangri-La has never been close.

3

It began with the possibility
that I could become a helicopter
and fly my way into success.
Who would have ever believed
from all those years of huffing
throughout my adolescence,
that I had become immune to jet fuel.
The only thing I lost were a few million
brain cells and my cognitive ability
to figure out what two plus two equals
when squared
or how many unpleasantries were necessary
to keep me moving above the clouds.

4

It began as a nightmare.
When every time I tried to whisper
into the ear of the woman beside me
wisteria leaves flew out my mouth.
If she had taken a look,
she would have seen
how in the back of my throat
the stems had taken root,
weaving themselves
like clasping hands.
What became loose wilted.
What remained attached
began to sprout
with the tips of the wisteria leaves
stepping out over my lips.
Soon all I could do was spit up
more and more wisteria
till I was a field of wisteria spreading.

5

It began during a commercial break,
after we ate licorice
and our teeth rotted
before falling out.
That's when we would gum kiss
our way toward excitement.
She had told me how happy
being toothless had made her,
and yet, it was then, day by day
she unglued, letter by letter her happiness.
Months later I thought
how you can't know something
is possible until it happens,
despite learning to live
with the unacceptable
workings of expiration dates.

6

It began when my body began creating its own memories.
That's when I got out the machete
to smooth out all the rough ends.
After that I blew up
balloons, hundreds of them
stuffing them in my closet.
What came over me, I can't say.
Perhaps a passing phase
like a mind found in a muddy ditch
alongside a pack of cigarettes.
Either way the balloons soon deflated
and just fell to the bottom of my closet and died.
That's when I got the phone call
from God asking "Whats up,
we haven't commiserated in a while."
And yes, I'm sure the voice said commiserated.
I'm certain.
So we commiserated like father and son,
with the son looking for answers
as to why the balloons had to die.
"Hell," God said, "they're just balloons."

7

It began years ago
before all the voices
in my head could make a decision.
I was an open book
with a terrible front cover.
People I had never met judged me.
If you looked from afar
you would see all my faults,
close up I was almost perfect,.
But everything changed
when I decided to believe in the perverse
and three days later I awoke
beside a woman
who knew how to kill.
We were damaged goods,
guilty of expectations.
And yet it was only a matter
of time before we realized
how damaged bodies
could still figure out
how to live within all their profanity.

8

It began when I lived
in a city with no speed limits,
every red light I ran
reminded me of the time
I dated my best friend's girl.
No one caught on
that I changed my accent
or practiced how to speak
with my mouth full.
I believed I was a complete person.
Secure, one with the self
as if a sage drew within.
Just before telling you all about this
you whispered the word "consequences."
I had to look up the word in the dictionary
but didn't know how to spell "apologies."
It was a color I was unfamiliar with.
Years later, the city
put up speed limit signs,
banning red lights
on every main road.

9

It began after the divorce.
Every time I looked at my reflection
it was difficult to put a name to the face.
There were so many forgotten possibilities
and I've never been able to figure out
what to do with all that unknowing.
Judge me, I'm okay with that,
but don't forget to judge yourself.
Everybody needs that.
What's worse than being told
you are not loved.
It's like falling to the ground
after your already on the ground
or giving up your wants
to hold onto everything you've ever wanted.
Different people do different things.
Take anything you want, take it all I say.
We are what we don't throw away.

10

It began when I received
a postcard from myself.
"There are no miracles," it read,
"without strings attached."
So excuse me
if I'm in the middle
of a mercy overdose.
It's easy to tell
when paranoia takes hold
and I refuse to say anything
about how I plan
to survive at all cost
no matter what the cost.
We're all two-bit part actors,
pretending to be someone else.
Right now I'm nameless.
I have complete anonymity.
I could be the stand-in,
asking for a hand out on the street corner
while doing the Watusi.

11

It began when I accidentally
walked into a room full of strangers
who used bandaids for hatchet wounds,
bleeding through their teeth
while sitting upright on wooden chairs,
measuring their lives with yardsticks
as if they were not sure
they had ever lived.
I soon got the idea it was a condition
that had been coming on for years.
No matter what I said
or how I carried on
the strangers in the room
paid me no mind.
They continued bleeding,
continued putting bandaids on their open wounds.

12

It began when you easily opened the door
to the back of my head
and you saw the forest in front of a raging fire.
The sun was coming up
so you thought nothing of the fact
that I was slowly disappearing.
I would have thought the same,
I'm no different
then the black carpenter ants
who walk into my house
full of resentment, hoping to escape
the tyranny of the garden fertilizer,
only to get stepped on.
But I've promised myself I'd change,
become a better man.
Someone who will consider
experiences as an irreplaceable
puzzle piece to his life.
A man with a dependable door
on the back of his head
that won't easily open,
no matter how invisible I eventually became.

Epilogue

It began when I went to the mailbox
and found a manila envelope from you.
How did you find me? I gave up
my name years ago
when it was still possible to become yourself,
despite the many disappointments.

Inside the envelope
sheets of blank copy paper
stapled together
as if it were a novella I needed
to meditate on,
rethink the characters
and keep track of their frailties.
Characters who needed to find
their own way to the epilogue
despite how lost they were.
That much I am certain.

About the Author

Michael Jemal was raised in Brooklyn, New York and now lives in the southern part of Rhode Island with his wife and son. He has studied with Stephen Dunn and B.J. Ward. He has been published in *Rattle*, *New Delta Review*, *Hiram Poetry Review* and in other publications.

www.ingramcontent.com/pod-product-compliance
Lightning Source LLC
LaVergne TN
LVHW091322080426

835510LV00007B/612